TRIUMPH OVER FEAR
THROUGH FAITH…

2 Corinthians 5:7 For we walk by faith, not by sight.

Victoria Grace

THANKS AND ACKNOWLEDGMENTS

I would like to take this time to thank and acknowledge the following important people in my life. My husband Joe for his constant encouragement, my daughters Davina and Danica as they serve as my inspirations. These two young ladies inspired me to keep my faith in the Lord Jesus Christ. As I looked at their innocent faces and watched them put their faith in Jesus Christ at the very young age has inspired me to grow and strengthen my faith in God.

This book came about in my daily devotion and reading the bible everyday. My fear of uncertainties leads me to have trust and have strong faith in God. To lay everything at the feet at the feet of Jesus Christ, that everything I need will provided and will be taken care of. For nothing will be impossible with God. I learned to walk by faith, not by sight. And whatever I ask in prayer, I will receive if I have faith.

ABOUT THE AUTHOR

Victoria Grace is a dedicated and faithful servant of the Lord Jesus Christ, Sunday school teacher (children and adults), Homegroup Leader, Life Coach, Christian Motivational Speaker, author, educator, and Ladies Group Facilitator. My experience in social services for twenty years has given me different perspectives in life and the world. In my free time, I like spending my time outdoors, and I enjoy nature and photography is my hobby. My writing derives from my everyday life experiences and is inspired by reading the words of God (Bible) everyday.

Through Jesus Christ, who gives me strength, I am able to face the reality of my past and lay everything down at the feet of Jesus. To forgive myself as the Lord has forgiven me. Through all my life's experiences, God is always there with me, loving me as it says in Jeremiah 29:11, "For I know the plans I have for you," declares the Lord, "plans to prosper you and not to harm you, plans to give you hope and a future."

PREFACE

Fear is looking at God through your problems. (2 Timothy 1:7 - For God hath not given us the spirit of fear; but of power, and of love, and of a sound mind.)

Faith is looking at your problems through God. (Hebrews 11:1 Now faith is confidence in what we hope for and assurance about what we do not see.)

We like to talk about fear …We all have it in us once a while, and it usually likes to get the best of us.

Fear is the act of not walking with the Lord Jesus Christ in our true Faith. When we worry about our jobs, our families, and our health, it is easy to fall into the fear of what am I going to do. You need to put your Faith and trust in Christ.

King David of Israel he conquered goliath and many other issues in life. When fear set in, he ran off to hide and not forgetting what God had done for him. We need to ask the same question: what to we do when fear is overwhelming us? Face the fear; look what God did for you prior to the fear. Remember that God is with you during that Fear. Most of all looks at what God has promised.

When you are in pure Faith with Jesus Christ, I mean really focus on HIM and what he has done for us and will continue. Then we should be in peace and joy that no matter what comes at us, Christ is in us by our Faith and will see us through that fearful issue we are in our lives.

Many times, the disciples showed their fear in situations because they really didn't rely on their Faith in Jesus. That's why he said a few times to them…You with little faith...

So just put all your focus and Faith in Jesus Christ, and he will fulfill that out come of your fears

To me fear means:

F- failing

E- emotion

A- and

R- response

In other words, if we do on our own, we will fail and respond in a matter that will not help us ...but continue to make us do the wrong thing.

Trust with all your heart and have Faith that Jesus Christ will be there for us always if we focus. And walk with him daily.

God bless all…Peace be in all…

Deuteronomy 31:6 Be strong and courageous. Do not fear or be in dread of them, for it is the Lord your God who goes with you. He will not leave you or forsake you.

To find what you seek in the road of life.... Leave no stones unturned and seek God daily through his words. Life has no smooth road for any of us; through, the roughness is not easy to tread on. Keep an even and steady pace. Let God be your guide in all that you do. As God promised, He will never leave you nor forsake you. Now see him not, yet believe, you rejoice with joy unspeakable and full of glory.

Proverbs 14:26-27 In the fear of the Lord is strong confidence: and his children shall have a place of refuge. The fear of the Lord is a fountain of life, to depart from the snares of death.

Don't try to get through the struggles of life by yourself because you will fail. Be strong in the Lord and keep your mind on Him. Commit to Him in prayer, meditate on His Word, and continually give Him praise.

Whenever fear starts to cripple you and doubts set in. Look to God and give to Him all your troubles and worries. Spend time with God and gaze upon His beautiful face. May we love God and dwell in the house of the Lord forever and ever. Our perspective in life will be positively good. As we let God guides us through our lives.

Without dependence on God and his guidance, even great ability is wasted.

Psalms 46:1-3 God is our refuge and strength, A very present help in trouble. 2 Therefore we will not fear, Even though the earth be removed, And though the mountains be carried into the midst of the sea; 3 Though its waters roar and be troubled, Though the mountains shake with its swelling.

We are often troubled by the uncertainties of life. The fear of mountains crumbling into the sea by a nuclear blast sometimes plays in our mind. God assured that even to the world's ends, we need not to fear. God is our refuge in the face of destruction. God gives us strength to face the uncertainties. God is not merely a temporary retreat; He is our eternal refuge.

Isaiah 65:1 "I revealed myself to those who did not ask for me; I was found by those who did not seek me. To a nation that did not call on my name, I said, 'Here am I, here am I.'"

When you are weary and feeling down. Reach out to God, and he will comfort you. When life seems so hard, pray to God; he will ease your burden. When darkness hovers you. Ask God for guidance; he will guide you. God will shine his face upon you to light your path to righteousness and holiness. When your light burns out. Ask God to be the light of your life. God will shine through you. You will become a light for others to follow. It's your time to shine. Shine bright with God's light in you.

Ezekiel 18:2 - 4 "Why do people use this proverb about the land of Israel: The children are punished for their fathers' sins? 3 As I live," says the Lord God, "you will not use this proverb anymore in Israel, 4 for all souls are mine to judge—fathers and sons alike—and my rule is this: It is for a man's own sins that he will die.

We often say we are being punished by God because of the sins of our ancestors, not our own. God does not punish us for someone else's sin; and we can not use their mistakes as an excuse for our sins. Although, we may suffer the effects and consequences of sins committed by those who came before us. Each person is accountable for his/her own actions.

Ephesians 2:10 For we are his workmanship, created in Christ Jesus for good works, which God prepared beforehand, that we should walk in them.

Just when you thought everything are fine and dandy, somehow God always find a way to remind you and to show you that He always commands your destiny.

Lest you get the wrong idea, you are not the sovereign master of your fate. Only God is sovereign. His sovereign control is called "providence." He has chosen to give you a free will, and He has created a moral universe in which the law of cause-and-effect is a reality. But God is God alone, and there are no "accidents" in the universe.

An all-wise, all-powerful God must have a plan, so it should be no surprise that the Bible speaks of a divine plan. God's plan, since it belongs to God, is holy, wise, and benevolent. The providence of God is working to bring about His original plan for creation.

Psalm 27:13 Yet I am confident I will see the Lord's goodness while I am here in the land of the living.

It doesn't matter what our circumstances are at the moment. Think positive, expect favorable results and situations, and circumstances will change accordingly. Positive thinking is a mental attitude. Positive mind anticipates happiness, joy, health, and a successful result. Let God transform and renew our way of thinking daily.

Psalms 73:25-26 Whom have I in heaven but You? And besides You, I desire nothing on earth. My flesh and my heart may fail, But God is the strength of my heart and my portion forever.

God is the source of your daily needs and life itself. He wants you to understand the importance of giving Him the glory and honor. There is nothing in this world that can fulfill our needs. Hence, you have nothing to worry about whether we are rich or poor, weak or strong, because God loves us just the same. Look at our life through heaven's eyes. Worship God in all that you do and wherever you go.

Romans 15:13 May the God of hope fill you with all joy and peace as you trust in him, so that you may overflow with hope by the power of the Holy Spirit.

Let the Holy Spirit fills you with hope, joy, and peace as you sometimes find yourselves feeling hopeless. Some circumstances in your lives can rob you of your joy and peace and leave us hopeless.

Many a time, we wish that certain events hadn't taken place. Sometimes, God allows unpleasant events to take place in order for us to rely on him to strengthen our faith. We will find eternal joy and inner peace through Jesus Christ, our Lord and Savior.

Isaiah 2:17 All the glory of mankind will bow low; the pride of men will lie in the dust, and the Lord alone will be exalted on high.

Sometimes, letting God be God is one of the hardest thing for Christians to do as our pride gets in the way of truly believing in Christ Jesus. To humble oneself before God is a sign of strength and obedience -- not a weakness. It is my prayer that we all have humble heart and spirit as we start our day of worship and thanksgiving.

Hebrews 13:16. Do not neglect to do good and to share what you have, for such sacrifices are pleasing to God.

God commanded us to do good to others and to all those who are unfortunate and unloved. For us to do a sacrificial love to others is pleasing and glorifying God. LOVE is one good thing we can do to anyone. LOVE is to sacrifice whatever it may to please God. LOVE is the answer to all that seemingly indefinable and unexplained circumstances in life. Let us love sacrificially as God loves us by scarifying his only begotten son, Jesus Christ. Love always.

John 14:1 Do not let your hearts be troubled. You believe in God; believe also in me.

We live with conflict, disappointment, and pain. We all experience hours of deep tragedy and times of severe trial, but He is with us. Whatever our trouble, whatever mess we are in, whatever anxiety or perplexity we have, just remember, the Lord Himself is there. As Christians, we need to always remember those who are less fortunate and always remind ourselves to be thankful for everything. Remember also that we are no better than others. No one is perfect here on earth. We must accept and love others in spite of their faults. We need to be sensitive of others' needs. Be encouraging. Be supportive.

***Deuteronomy 4:9** "Only take care, and keep your soul diligently, lest you forget the things that your eyes have seen, and lest they depart from your heart all the days of your life. Make them known to your children and your children's children.*

As we look and reflect about life; our perspective may change for the better.

In the eyes of a child, there is joy; there is laughter, there is hope, a chance to shape the future. There is no greater teacher than a look in the eyes of a child. We may look at each child as our greatest teacher. Children are precious gifts from God. Teach them well and love them, for they are our future. When love we give our children they show and find love in the world around them. Let us not exasperate our children. Let us teach them the ways of the Lord....our Savior Jesus Christ.

Psalms 68:19"Praise be to the Lord, to God our Savior, who daily bears our burdens."

Each day, we must deal with our share of earthly burdens. As we face these burdens, the Lord is there to help us bear them. Each morning, praise God for the strength He will send us today; it is as sure as the sunrise. We should feel an overwhelming awe as we kneel before the Lord. Surrounding us with countless signs of His majesty. Unlimited power and unspeakable majesty leave us breathless in His presence. When we catch our breath, praise God.

2 Timothy 2:22 Flee the evil desires of youth and pursue righteousness, faith, love, and peace, along with those who call on the Lord out of a pure heart.

Running away is sometimes considered cowardly. But wise people realize that removing oneself physically from temptations often prudent. Perhaps, there are times when we experience a recurring temptation that is difficult to resist. Knowing when to run is as important as knowing when and how to fight. May we surround ourselves with righteousness, faith, love, and peace.

***1 Thessalonians 3:7** We are greatly comforted, dear brothers, in all of our suffering here, now that we know you are standing firm and true to the Lord.*

In the midst of persecution and pressure, we as believers, should encourage each other. Express thanks and support to those who are wavering in the faith to help others. It's a great joy for Christians to build each other up. It is my prayer that we yearn for God's love, hope, peace, and wisdom. That we may love others in spite of.....We often think wealth is having material things and money. Not true. Our true treasures are in heaven, family (children especially), and friends. Good friend/s are often hard to come by; if you find one true friend, he/she is a treasure to cherish. All in all, there is one and only true friend, our Lord Jesus Christ....Oh, what a friend we have in Jesus....

Hebrews 13:2 Be not forgetful to entertain strangers: for thereby some have entertained angels unawares.

This scripture is a reminder that we should treat all people well. It reminds us that everyone we meet may be an angel sent from God, even though we may not be aware of it. This admonition hearkens back to the Old Testament, which tells of several incidences of angelic visitation. Every stranger we meet is surely not an angel, but every stranger we meet is surely made in the image of God, so we need to treat every stranger accordingly.

2 Peter 3:10-11 But the day of the Lord will come as a thief in the night, in which the heavens will pass away with a great noise, and the elements will melt with fervent heat; both the earth and the works that are in it will be burned up. Therefore, since all these things will be dissolved, what manner of persons ought you to be in holy conduct and godliness?

Do we spend more time acquiring possessions and fame, or are we striving to develop Christ like characters? We must not sit and wait for His return but live in realization that the time is short and we have work to do. Let us be ready to meet Christ any time as if He is coming today, yet plan our course of service as if He may not return for many years. We should put our confidence in what is lasting and eternal.

Psalms 14:2 The Lord looks down from heaven on all mankind to see if there are any who understand, any who seek God.

God alone is perfect in every way. We are but mere creatures created by God. God and God alone created all things we call our own. Always seek God with our heart, mind, and soul. For He alone is worthy to be praised. Love God, and we'll understand his ways to love others.

Psalm 59:16 - 17 But I will sing of your strength, in the morning I will sing of your love; for you are my fortress, my refuge in times of trouble.17 You are my strength, I sing praise to you; you, God, are my fortress, my God on whom I can rely.

We live in a world where unfairness and injustice seem to triumph. The rich get richer, and the poor get poorer. When wrong seems right, and the darkness hovers us relentlessly. Standing up for is right, is a fight we battle each day. Giving up is sometimes the best, and succumbing to the lure of unrighteousness. Our eyes become a fountain of tears. Our hearts heavily burden with sadness and sorrow. Through it all, we will discover God's everlasting love. God also comforts us during our struggles and distress. Stand firm and trust in the Lord God Almighty.

Psalms 119:105. Your word is a lamp to guide my feet and a light for my path.

Each day brings joy and sadness, trials and tribulations. Our God is an awesome God. When we let God's words guide us, we will get through life's struggles... Our burden will be light, and he restores our spirit. Have faith in God; he controls everything that goes in our lives. Keep smiling and keep loving.

James 1:12 Blessed is the one who perseveres under trial because, having stood the test, that person will receive the crown of life that the Lord has promised to those who love him.

Our life is God's instruents so others may see His great love and mercy. Our gracious Father in Heaven place us here to be His representation. Let us live a godly life that is pleasing to God alone.

Our daily walk may not always be pleasant; in this world, we will have troubles, but God's love overcomes the world.

Psalms 112:4 Light arises in the darkness for the upright; He is gracious and compassionate and righteous.

Often, we ignore God's words to us as we seek pleasure for our own. Hence, God allows us to make mistakes of decisions we made as we misinterpreted what God is telling us. We often misunderstood the signs God put forth before us as we forgo to pursue what we want instead of God's wants for us.

Through repentance. May God show us mercy and that we will be forgiven. We sometimes create darkness in our lives. When we do things that we shouldn't be doing, life can become complicated.

Psalm 138:6 Though the Lord is exalted, he looks kindly on the lowly; though lofty, he sees them from afar.

As we watch from the distant, as to what happening in our community and the world. It is hard to fathom and understand the pains and sufferings these people are going through. No one is immune to pain and suffering. Let's continually pray that in the midst of calamity, people around the world will find God's love and peace.

Psalm 107:8 Let them give thanks to the Lord for his unfailing love and his wonderful deeds for mankind,

Life presents so many challenges every day, whether at work, home, or just a normal day. One thing is for sure: God is in control of everything. No matter what challenges, we face we can be confident God is with us.

Life is a mystery, but God said abide in me, and I'll abide in you. Don't dwell in the past; live and enjoy the present, and look forward to tomorrow. God is not yet finished shaping our tomorrow.

Proverbs 4:23 Above all else, guard your heart, for everything you do flows from it.

We all want satisfaction in life. Therefore, we neglect to follow God's direction. Our feelings of love and desire dictate how we live. The best time to learn about right and wrong is before temptation besets us. We often find time to do what we enjoy. Therefore, we need to make sure that our affections are leading us to the path of righteousness. Put boundaries on our desires by not going after everything we see. Keep our eyes fixed upon Jesus, our Lord and Savior.

Isaiah 41:10 "So do not fear, for I am with you; do not be dismayed, for I am your God. I will strengthen you and help you; I will uphold you with my righteous right hand."

May yesterday taught you a lesson about life; ourselves, and about the world. Lessons that will impact and shape our today and tomorrow. May the mistakes you made along the way, taught you a lesson or two to a path of a better tomorrow. May the pains and sorrows you leave behind lead you to happiness and joy. Because Jesus Christ lives, you can face tomorrow and face uncertain days.

You may not know what tomorrow brings, but you can be confident that God holds you lovingly and guides you towards a path of righteousness. You have new hopes, new opportunities, and new challenges ahead. Make the most of today joyous and blissful as you continue to glorify God.

2 Samuel 22:7 In my distress I called to the LORD; I called out to my God. From his temple, he heard my voice; my cry came to his ears.

During our difficulties, call out to God and have faith. Even if you face what seems to be calamity, during your troubles, cry out to God. Let your emotions come through to Him. And be assured that He will both hear and save you. God hears, and He understands. Have faith in the Lord Jesus Christ.

Jeremiah 24:7 I will give them a heart to know me, that I am the LORD. They will be my people, and I will be their God, for they will return to me with all at their heart.

God's grace is infinite, and His faithfulness is so great. Let us be thankful and enjoy each day God has given us. A day to discover God's blessings. In all that we do, in all our heartaches and pains, remember God is always faithful. Therefore, let us trust in him alone.

1 John 1:7 "But if we walk in the light, as he is in the light, we have fellowship with one another, and the blood of Jesus his Son cleanses us from all sin."

Real cleansing from your sins came from Jesus Christ, our Lord and Savior. The Lamb of God who takes away the sins of the world. You will never fully understand this that Jesus Christ died because of your sins. When you identify yourselves with him, his death becomes yours. You will discover that he has fully paid the penalty of your sins, his blood has cleansed you. As Jesus rose from the grave, you rise to a new life of fellowship with the Lord Jesus Christ.

1 John 1:5 This is the message we have heard from Him and announce to you, that God is Light, and in Him there is no darkness at all.

Light (faith) represents what is good, pure, true, and holy. Darkness (fear) represents what is unholy and ungodly. To say God is light, it means that God is perfect and true. God alone can guide you from darkness. Be true to God, to yourselves, and to others. May your light shine truly to the path of righteousness and holiness. May you love truly with God's love in your heart. May your light and your love, truth, and holiness shine brighter as you continue to walk in the light (faith) and love (hope) of God.

Psalm 68:19 Praise be to the Lord, to God our Savior, who daily bears our burdens."

Each day, we must deal with our share of earthly burdens. As we face these burdens, the Lord is there to help us bear them. Each morning, praise God for the strength He will send us today; it is as sure as the sunrise. We should feel an overwhelming awe as we kneel before the Lord. Surrounding us with countless signs of His majesty. Unlimited power and unspeakable majesty leave us breathless in His presence.

Psalms 141:4 Do not let my heart be drawn to what is evil so that I take part in wicked deeds along with those who are evildoers; do not let me eat their delicacies.

Temptations are always around us; thus, we need to pray that God changes our heart's desires. Evil acts begin with evil desires. Ask God to take away our lustful and envious desires. Let God transform our hearts and renew our minds.

When we fear the Lord, we develop love. We no longer fear life here on earth. We are more concerned about life that we are going to have in heaven. Be a fountain of life.

Deuteronomy 4:9 "Only take care, and keep your soul diligently, lest you forget the things that your eyes have seen, and lest they depart from your heart all the days of your life. Make them known to your children and your children's children—

As we look and reflect about life; our perspective may change for the better.

In the eyes of a child, there is joy, there is hope, a chance to shape the future. There is no greater teacher than a look in the eyes of a child. We may look at each child as our greatest teacher. Children are precious gifts from God. Teach them well and love them, for they are our future. When love we give our children they show and find love in the world around them. Let us not exasperate our children. Let us teach them the ways of the Lord....our Savior Jesus Christ.

Judges 6:23, "But the LORD said to him, 'Peace! Do not be afraid.'"

Our position is changing constantly. It may be in our responsibilities as a parent, a new job, at home, or in our calling. In this new place, our loving Heavenly Father wants to show us His perspective of who He is and what He wants to do in us and through us. Open our hearts past the pain of change and ask God to change our perspective to see Him in this new place.

God changed my position to change my perspective. Moves, job changes, places I have held in people's hearts. Each change brings another opportunity for God to change my perspective. Like the disciples, I can see Him in new ways. I haven't seen Him before: my Provider, my Healer, my Light and Salvation, my True Love.

Psalms 73:25-26 Whom have I in heaven but You? And besides You, I desire nothing on earth. My flesh and my heart may fail, But God is the strength of my heart and my portion forever.

God is the source of our daily needs and life itself. He wants us to understand the importance of giving Him the glory and honor. There is nothing in this world that can fulfill our needs. Hence. We have nothing to worry about whether we are rich or poor, weak or strong, because God loves us just the same. Look at our life through heaven's eyes. Let us worship God in all that we do and wherever we go.

Psalms 62:5 My soul, wait thou only upon God; for my expectation is from him.

Expectations....We often have unrealistic expectations of others and of ourselves. And usually, when that happens, the outcome isn't so great. We feel disappointed, hurt, and resentful. Why is it that accepting things as they are and not having expectations is difficult to do. A battle we can never win is fighting within own being as we set our hearts and minds to greater expectations. May we expect less from others and from ourselves but strive for a better good.

Matthew 6:33 Seek the Kingdom of God above all else and live righteously, and he will give you everything you need.

Seek and trust God always, for He will never leave us nor forsake us. God alone can know our tomorrow, our heart's desires and wants. We are God's most valuable creation, and He loves us so. Let us live a righteous life, and to God alone we cast our cares and burdens. God knows our needs and provides accordingly. You are God's most valuable creation.

Malachi 1:2 I have loved you deeply, said the Lord....

God loves you so much even when you neglect or disobey him. God has great blessings to bestow upon us when you are faithful to him, as his love never ends.

Because God loves you so much, he wants you to live a life that is pleasing to him. The kind of living and relationship he wants to have with us. What you give and how you live reflect the sincerity of your love for God.

Job 42:2 I know that you can do all things; no purpose of yours can be thwarted.

Strong and independent people often find themselves feeling alone when the going is tough in their own life. They may be surrounded by people whom they walked with when their journey was tough. However, independent people seem to not have the courage to ask for guidance from others. Perhaps, because they are known to be strong, and they rely on no one but God alone. Have faith in the Lord Jesus Christ.

Galatians 5:22 But the Holy Spirit produces this kind of fruit in our lives: love, joy, peace, patience, kindness, goodness, faithfulness,

Your words and actions define our true characters when the going is tough and when you are faced with adversities. May you always remember to think first before you speak. Use kind and encouraging words towards others, especially to those who are unkind and uncaring.

You can learn to follow God by meditating on God's law and have faith in God's words. Spend time reading and thinking about God's words.

1 Corinthians 15:58 Therefore, my dear brothers and sisters, stand firm. Let nothing move you. Always give yourselves fully to the work of the Lord because you know that your labor in the Lord is not in vain.

As you do God's work, it often requires your full commitment and dedication. God knows your heart and your motivation when you are doing service to him. Are you pleasing God, yourselves, or others? Let us examine ourselves to the true motives of our helping and serving others. May your effort to help others is pure, without hidden agenda, and without reservation. Do all things to please God alone.

Psalm 5:5 Therefore, proud sinners will not survive your searching gaze, for how you hate their evil deeds.

God's love is complete. It reaches every corner of your experience. It continues to the length of your lives. It reaches to the depths of discouragement and despair. It covers and reaches out to the whole world. It rises to the height of your celebration and elation. When you feel alone and isolated, remember that you can never be lost in God's love. And to know the love of Jesus Christ, which surpasses knowledge, that you may be filled up to all the fullness of God.

Psalms 128:1 - 2 Blessings on all who reverence and trust the Lord---on all who obey Him. Their reward shall be prosperity and happiness.

May you find ways to be in constant obedient to God's leading in your lives. We are but mere human being, humbled by the grace and mercy. God loves you in spite of and regardless of what you have done. When you trust and obey as, there is no other way but to trust and obey.

May the Lord continually bless you with heaven's blessings as well as human joy.

Philippians 4:6-7 Be anxious for nothing, but in everything by prayer and supplication, with thanksgiving, let your requests be made known to God; and the peace of God, which surpasses all understanding, will guard your hearts and minds through Christ Jesus.

Real peace comes from knowing that God is in control of everything: our hopes and our destiny. Ultimate joy comes from Christ's dwelling in us. Imagine never having to worry about anything. Do we want to worry less? Then, we should pray more.

Colossians 3:23 Whatever you do, work at it with all your heart, as working for the Lord, not for human masters,

In all that you do, do it cheerfully. Let us not expect anything in return. Be a servant of God with heart that is so loving and giving with love. We must do all as if we are doing it for the Lord Almighty and not because we want to impress others. Our motivation to do something or our service for others should be pleasing to God alone.

Psalm 27:1 The Lord is my light and my salvation.

Fear is a dark shadow that envelops us and ultimately imprison us within ourselves. Each of us, at one time or another we fear rejection, uncertainty, sickness, or even death. But if we remember the bright, liberating light of God that brings salvation, we can conquer and dispel fear through Jesus Christ, our Saviour and Lord.

Psalm 27:1 The Lord is my light and my salvation—

Fear is a dark shadow that envelops us and ultimately imprison us within ourselves. Each of us at one time or another we fear rejection, uncertainty, sickness or even death. But if we remember the bright liberating light of God that brings salvation we can conquer and dispel fear.

Psalm 73:26 My flesh and my heart may fail, but God is the strength of my heart and my portion forever."

Sometimes life seems so good, and all is awesomely beautiful. We are joyous and elated that our hearts soar in happiness. Other times, the ground beneath our feet is crumbling. It appears we are falling into the abyss of nothingness.

There seems to be nothing in between. Life instant mystery. God alone is the author of our life. He knows our beginning and our ending. Therefore, abiding and trusting God in all that we do is a must.

When we face trials and tribulations, let us rejoice. Seeking always God's guidance and His kingdom. And we will dwell in the realm of His glory forever. There is no greater joy but to rest our heavily laden heart in God's loving arms. In Christ alone, our hope is found.

HAVE FAITH ALWAYS....

Faith caused Abel to worship God.

Faith caused Enoch to walk with God.

Faith caused Noah work with God.

Faith caused Abraham to wait on God.

A Simple Sinner's Prayer ("For all have sinned and fall short of the glory of God" Romans 3:23)

Dear Heavenly Father, I come to you in the name of Jesus Christ. I acknowledge to You that I am a sinner, and I am sorry for my sins and the life that I have lived; I need your forgiveness.

I believe that your only Son, Jesus Christ, shed His precious blood on the cross at Calvary and died for my sins, and I am now willing to repent, confess, and turn from my sin. You said in the bible that if I confess the Lord our God and believe in my heart that God raised Jesus from the dead, I shall be saved.

I confess Jesus Christ as my Lord and my Saviour. With my heart, I believe that God raised Jesus from the dead. This very moment, I accept Jesus Christ as my own personal Savior and according to His Word, right now I am saved. Amen.

www.ingramcontent.com/pod-product-compliance
Lightning Source LLC
Chambersburg PA
CBHW050301120526
44590CB00016B/2445